MODELING
in Clay, Plaster and Papier-mâché

Richard Slade

MODELING
in Clay, Plaster and Papier-mâché

ILLUSTRATED WITH PHOTOGRAPHS

Lothrop, Lee & Shepard Co., Inc.
NEW YORK

Contents

MODELING
in Clay, Plaster and Papier-mâché

1. Clay Modeling

MATERIALS AND TOOLS

A clay that can be used for the models in this book is Boneware Self-hardening Clay. Provided the models are kept small, this clay does not need firing. It will dry hard without cracking, can be very satisfactorily painted, and is excellent for beginners in clay work. It is packed in five-pound lots in plastic bags and can be obtained in stores that sell artists' materials. A list of material sources and a note on firing clay will be found at the end of the book.

The plastic bag in which the clay is packed should be opened carefully, so as not to tear the bag unnecessarily. When you have removed the clay you need, seal the bag again. This will keep the unused clay in a workable condition indefinitely. As an additional safeguard, you can put another plastic bag over the one containing the clay. These bags are available in supermarkets and variety stores.

Use a fairly large, smooth, flat board, about eighteen inches by fifteen inches, as a worktable. Five-ply wood is very suitable. It can be easily cleaned and stored after use.

Most of the modeling is done by hand, but one or two modeling tools are helpful. These can be bought at an art-supply store or produced at home. Some homemade ones are shown in Figure 6; they were made by looping pliable wire over the end of a dowel and taping it down firmly.

It is best to use a rolling pin to make slabs, although a length of broomstick will do the job. See that it is really smooth all around; otherwise, the surface of the slab will be uneven. When making slabs, you will want two short lengths of wood, about half an inch thick, on which to rest the roller.

A hand bowl, a small sponge, preferably a natural one, a towel or rag for drying your hands, and an old table knife for cutting the clay are also necessary.

Since the clay comes ready for modeling, do not add any water to it, unless it is indicated for joining purposes, and then only sparingly. Use the water and sponge for keeping your hands clean (after rinsing off the clay always dry them before continuing to model), and for keeping your tools clean, as you do not want clay to dry hard on them. If the clay sticks to the knife when you cut it, dip the knife in water.

You will need a hammer and a small saw when you are making frames, and a pair of pliers will be required for making wire armatures.

All kinds of things can be brought into service to create original designs on clay. Fork prongs, spoon handles, dowels, pencils, bottle caps, buttons, pieces of pipe, pieces of rope are just a few of the objects you can use. Some advice on how to use them will be given later.

Small clay models look nice when they are painted, so we can conclude our list with a brush or two and some paints.

BASIC SHAPES

With an idea in our head of what we want to make we can take a piece of clay, knead it a bit, and begin modeling. However, in order to help you make a start, a simple method of modeling clay is set out here. You will find as you become interested in clay work that you will develop your own way of modeling. One thing to remember at the outset is not to make your models too thin or spindly, or they will break easily. Rather, keep them on the sturdy side.

The basic shapes suggested are the cube, the sphere or ball, the cone, the coil, and the slab, in that order (see Figure 1).

Models from cubes

Take a piece of clay about the size of a tennis ball and shape it roughly into a ball. Cut a cube from this with your knife; then, using the surface of your worktable and a small, flat piece of wood, shape the cube as accurately as possible. Avoid sharp edges and round the corners slightly as that is more in keeping with clay work.

Paperweights are attractive little models to make

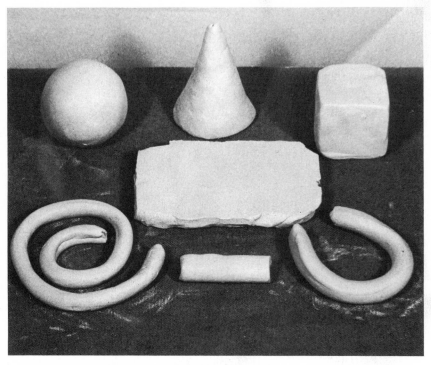

1. Basic shapes for modeling in clay

from small cubes. They can be decorated by pressing designs on them. For example, a design can be made on the sides of the cube by pressing a piece of cord on it at regular intervals. Or imprints can be made with the end of a pencil.

If you find that the clay is too sticky to take a clean imprint, let it dry out for a few hours until you are able to make a clear impression with the printing object.

Should you wish to paint a design on the cube, let it dry for a day or two first. It will still be soft enough to take an impression of the pencil point, which will give you good guide lines for painting. How to make a design on clay will be found on page 17.

To make a bowl from a cube, press in the center of the clay with your thumbs and mold it slowly into a bowl shape.

Other simple models are ashtrays and containers for matches.

2. A small bowl modeled from a sphere

Models from spheres

Decide on what kind of object you want to make and prepare the clay accordingly. A number of small balls can be modeled into an animal figure, for example.

To make nicely rounded clay balls, first roll the clay on the worktable and then between the palms of the hands. Rotate both hands and exert only a gentle pressure on the clay. With a little practice this will bring it to the required shape.

When joining two clay surfaces, score or roughen the clay where the join is to be made and dampen it with your sponge. This will help to knit the clay together and make a secure join.

The body of an animal may be left spherical, and the other balls of clay molded into different parts of the figure, the ball shapes being easy to start from.

The model of a human being can be very simply made from four balls without altering their shape, except to flatten the bottom one into a base. When making a model like this, it is important to have the joins secure.

Models from cones

The cone is a little harder to fashion than either the cube or the sphere. Make a short, thick coil, then press down on one end as you roll it; lift it up and bang the base on the worktable. This will give you a rough cone shape. Then it is just a matter of shaping the clay further with your hands. Look down on the cone to see that the top is in the middle.

Attractive doll-like figures can be made from small cones. First, place a round, flat piece on top of the cone as a ruffle and then, without altering the shape, put a ball of clay on top of that for the head. Shape a tiny cone for the hat, add small pellets of clay for nose and buttons, and you have a clown.

To make a small bulb or plant pot from a cone, press down the top with your thumbs to make a hole in the center and work out the base with your thumbs.

Angel figures can be made by adding wings. Paperweights should have a small projection at the top for grasping. Decorate with imprints or paint or both.

Models from coils

Make some coils on your worktable like those in Figure 1 by rolling out the clay with your hands. The process of making small bowls and vases from coils is not too difficult. A good way to start is to use an object like a glass with straight sides to help you.

Make a base of coils one coil wider than the base of the glass. Stand the glass on top of it and wind coils around the glass until they are about two inches high. Do not make the sides too high or they will collapse.

With your fingers or a modeling tool smooth the outside of the bowl, joining the coils as you go. Remove the glass carefully and go over the inside of the bowl as you did the outside.

3. *A bowl modeled from coils*

Make your next small bowl without using the glass. Bowls of various shapes and sizes can be made in this way. First make the base the required shape and then build up the coils on top of it.

Animal shapes can also be made with coils, using one coil for the body and another for each pair of legs. Put a coil over the body rather than under it and then model it into the body coil.

Models from slabs

Many flat shapes can be cut from a slab of clay and decorated with imprints and painting. Let us begin with a six-inch-square tile.

The clay must first be rolled out in the form of a slab. To do this, place two narrow pieces of wood, about a foot long and half an inch thick, on your worktable, and press out some clay between them. Then, resting the rolling pin or a similar roller on the wood, roll the clay flat.

Half an inch of wood will give you the right thickness for a tile (see Figure 4). Anything much thinner is liable to break easily. You will soon learn to judge how much clay is needed. If you have to add more clay, then

4. Rolling out a slab

pick up the slab, knead the fresh clay into it, and start again.

You may find that the clay slab sticks to the work-table when you want to lift it. This problem is overcome by putting a sheet of waxed paper underneath the clay before rolling it. The paper and clay will come off the board cleanly, and you can remove the paper when necessary.

Cut out a square of card six inches by six inches, place it on the prepared slab, and cut around it with a knife. Before attempting to lift the tile, remove the surplus clay and return it to the plastic bag.

Let the tile dry out for a day or two until the surface is hard, but not too hard to be easily indented with a pencil tip.

Make a six-inch square on a piece of writing paper and draw your design for the tile on it. If you wish you can trace a design onto it, but do not make it too complicated. When you have the design you want, cut out the square and tape it on top of the tile. Go over the design firmly with your pencil and an imprint will be made on the clay. You can check on your progress by loosening one edge of the paper. Paint the design after the tile has completely dried out.

Imprints can also be made on the clay while it is still soft.

These tiles can be put to use as stands for flowerpots, teapots, and so on. To prevent scratches on furniture, a tile to be used as a stand should be backed with a piece of felt, which can be glued in place.

Tiles of many shapes can be made in this manner.

To make a plant pot from slabs, first cut card patterns as follows: one four-by-four-inch card (bottom) and two three-by-three-inch cards and two four-by-three-inch cards (sides). Lay them out on clay slabs and cut around them. Remember to keep to half-inch thicknesses.

Arrange the sides around the bottom piece to make a pot three and half inches high (it will shrink to less than that when dry). Score and dampen the clay where the joins are to be made, and smooth over the joins with your fingers inside and outside the pot.

As before, let the clay dry out a little and then add imprints or a design you have drawn yourself. Let it dry thoroughly before painting.

Slabs can be wrapped around cans or similar containers to make round pots. Choose a round can or jar with straight sides. Trace around the base onto some paper. Cut the circle out; fold it in half to find the diameter, then in half again to get the radius. Measure the radius and add half an inch to that figure. With a compass draw a circle that size on paper and cut it out. This will be the pattern for the base of the clay pot. It will be half an inch larger all around to allow for the thickness of the side slab.

Next wrap a piece of paper around the can and cut it to size. This will give you the height and circumference of the pot. Place this piece of paper on another larger piece. Draw a second rectangle two inches longer than the first one and cut it out. This will be your pattern for the side wall of the pot. You will find that you need at

5. *A round pot from slabs*

least two extra inches of clay to go around the can completely. Any surplus can be cut away neatly with a knife and the ends of the clay scored before joining them.

The can should now be wrapped in a piece of paper that covers the sides only and projects an inch or two above them. The paper will prevent the clay from sticking and assist in its removal from the can.

Now stand the can in the center of the round clay base and have the rectangle of clay ready to wrap around it. Score the bottom edge of the rectangle where it is to be joined to the base, and score the projecting part of the base and dampen it slightly. Put the clay around the can and join it where it meets. Smooth the joins together with your fingers.

Let the clay dry for an hour or two, then remove the can. The can must be removed fairly soon, because the clay shrinks.

Attractive pots for plants can be made in this way.

Experimenting with various other shapes

When the time comes for experimenting with clay shapes, make up some coils, cubes, spheres, and cones. Arrange them in different ways on the worktable. When something pleases you, put it together into a model or figure.

Try modeling with a single piece of clay. You might draw a pencil sketch beforehand of what you want to make. Keep it simple, and keep the parts fairly thick.

MODELING ON AN ARMATURE

An armature, in this instance, is a structure that will hold the clay in place. It can be of wood or metal or both. For our kind of modeling pliable wire is probably the best.

The wire is twisted into a sort of skeleton of the figure or model that you wish to make. It is then fastened to a piece of board with nails or staples.

Make a number of small balls or pellets, press them onto the wire, and build up the shape. When you are close to what you want, finish the figure with a modeling tool.

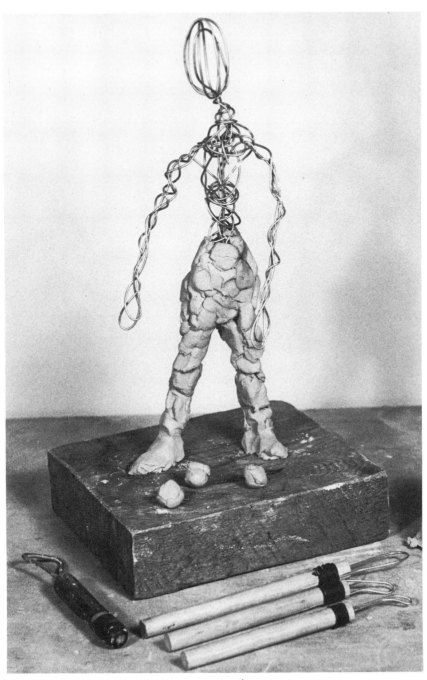

6. *Modeling clay on an armature* / *Homemade tools*

2. Plaster Modeling

MATERIALS AND TOOLS

Different kinds of plaster are used for different purposes. The best kind to use for the type of modeling we have in mind here is called White Casting Plaster. It is available from most large art-supply stores or can be ordered from Sculpture House, Inc., which is listed at the back of the book. This plaster comes in five-, twenty-five, fifty-, and one-hundred-pound packages. A twenty-five-pound bag will last a long time.

Always keep plaster in a dry place; any dampness will cause it to harden.

A plastic bowl or bucket is recommended for mixing plaster. Surplus plaster can be left to harden in a plastic container and it will knock out easily afterward, leaving the container clean. For mixing small amounts of plaster use a discarded plastic bottle. Cut the top off the bottle, and you have a handy container, which can be thrown away when you are finished with it.

Do not allow plaster to go down a sink or drain, or blockage may result. Instead, wrap waste in newspaper and put it in the trash can. If you do have to rinse plaster from your hands, do it in a bucket, and let the plaster settle in the bucket before pouring off the water.

A wooden or plastic spoon is handy for measuring and stirring. Scoops are easily fashioned from plastic bottles.

Old scissors make ideal cutters for wire mesh and tin. Some of the tools already mentioned for clay work, such as a hammer and pliers, are necessary when making frames and armatures.

Linoleum for frames is available from an art-supply store or, in scraps, from any store selling kitchen linoleum. Tools with which to cut the linoleum can be obtained in most art-supply stores.

A scriber, which might be an old dart or a compass point, is useful for marking out designs on plaster.

Plasticine, a soft clay, will come in handy for making molds.

It is also good to have a piece of board to work on as with clay modeling.

MIXING PLASTER

Put some water in a container and sprinkle the plaster onto the water. It will probably take more plaster than you think to make a good, creamy mixture, which is just about right for modeling. But watch for the plaster to rise in a small island above the water. Then stir it thoroughly to get out air bubbles. Do not try to rush the job; mix it slowly and add the plaster carefully.

Whatever you intend to make, the plaster must be the last thing you prepare. Everything must be ready when the plaster is mixed, and it must be used right away, because it dries quickly. So if, for example, you are making a plaster tile, have the frame into which the plaster is to be poured ready and handy.

Finally, when working with plaster, put on some old clothes, or roll up your sleeves and wear an apron. Also, find a place where no one minds a mess on the floor. You might think plaster had legs, it wanders around so much.

MAKING TILES

Tiles are probably the easiest thing to make with plaster, and although they are simple, they give a great deal of satisfaction when finished and decorated. Tiles can be used for many purposes, as stands for various articles or as wall decorations. If they are used as stands, glue a piece of felt on the back as with the clay tiles to prevent table marks and scratches.

To make a six-inch-square tile, fit up a square frame out of wood half an inch thick—half-inch balsa will do— on a plywood or hardboard base. Nail the frame to the base and leave the nails protruding so that the frame can be taken apart easily. The inside measurements of the frame have to measure six inches by six inches (see Figure 7), and the tiles should be at least half an inch thick.

Mix the plaster to a creamy consistency and pour it into the prepared frame. Knock the worktable to make the plaster settle in the frame and to free air bubbles.

7. *A frame for casting a plaster tile and the cast tile*

Let the plaster dry for thirty minutes and remove the frame. Should a piece of the tile come away with the frame, make it good with a little fresh plaster. The edges can be trimmed with a knife if necessary.

A design can be transferred to the plaster when it is dry by first drawing the design on thin paper, securing the paper to the tile with Scotch Tape and then going over the drawing firmly with a pencil. Do not have the pencil point too sharp or it may tear the paper. The imprint that will be made in the plaster can be deepened further, if desired, by going over it with a sharp metal point.

A design can also be gouged out, and a linoleum-cutting tool is used for this. One way to finish the tile is to fill the gouged parts with a colored plaster.

To make colored plaster, add ink or paint to the water you mix it with. Pour the colored plaster into the prepared design. Any surplus can be partly removed im-

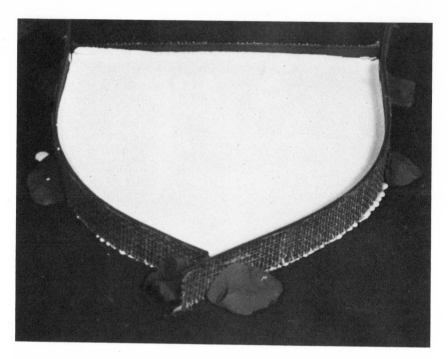

8. Casting a plaster shield

mediately and the rest when the plaster is dry. Finally rub down the tile with fine sandpaper.

MAKING SHIELDS

These are made similarly to the tiles, but instead of a wooden frame, use a linoleum strip for the shape. The strip should be at least half an inch wide.

If the outline of the shield is first drawn on the baseboard, the linoleum strip can be arranged along the outline. Keep the strip in position with pieces of plasticine as in Figure 8. If you find that the plaster runs out underneath the strip, seal it all along its length with plasticine or other clay. However, if the plaster is not made too runny there should be no danger of this.

When the shield has been painted, it can be mounted on a piece of board and hung on the wall (see Figure 15).

FIGURES OVER ARMATURES

Armatures for plaster work can be made from wire, perforated zinc, wire mesh, screening, and so on. The armature will need a support or base while you put on the plaster, but it can be removed afterward.

To apply plaster to a wire armature, first wrap the wire in one-inch bandage or in strips of cotton cloth. This will hold the plaster in place.

If the plaster is thick, you will have to work quickly. It can be applied with a flat knife and fingers. However, if you make it fairly thin, it can be put on with a brush.

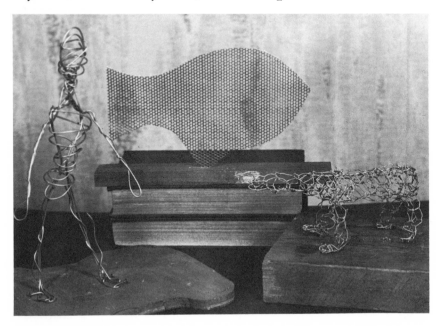

9. Three kinds of wire armature used for plaster modeling

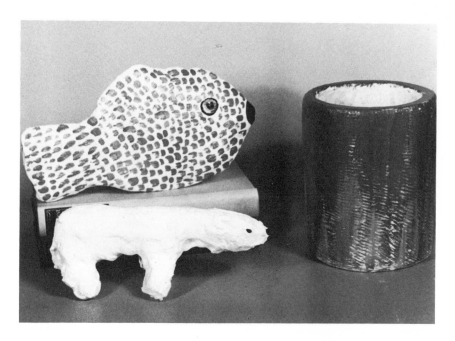

10. *Fish and bear made on armatures with plaster. Finished
clay pot, made out of slabs*

Wash the brush the minute you have finished using it.

Try making figures from string and rope. Dip them in colored plaster and hang them up to dry. Carefully remove unwanted bits of plaster from the figures when they are dry.

SIMPLE CASTING IN RELIEF

Small food containers of cardboard, foil cake pans, cardboard boxes, and so on are suitable for this kind of work.

A container is first half filled with plasticine or other clay. The clay is then impressed with a design made by such objects as the end of a knife handle, the rim of a small can, the end of a spool, or whatever you decide on.

Small objects like buttons can be laid on the clay and left protruding from it after being pressed into it slightly to secure them. Plaster is then poured in to fill the rest of the container.

When the plaster is dry, lift the clay and plaster together from the container. Then pull the clay from the plaster. This will give you a plaque with a sculptured

11. *Cast tile ready for decoration*

effect, which might be finished in a metallic paint, mounted on a piece of board, and hung on the wall.

This method can be applied to larger castings in relief. Slab reliefs can be made by using a shoe box and making the clay and the plaster considerably thicker. Designs can be tooled on the clay before pouring in the plaster.

12. *Preparation for casting a plaster figure from a model made of plasticine*

CASTING A FIGURE

For this let the figure be a simple model from plasticine. You might get an idea for the figure from primitive sculpture; the one in Figure 12 was based on an Aztec god. Keep it as simple as possible; that is, avoid fine detail and make the model squat and solid.

You will need small pieces of tin, technically known as *shims*. These can be readily cut from a thin tin box

13. Plasticine model with shims inserted

with a pair of scissors. The shims are pushed halfway into the plasticine figure, beginning on one side of the figure and working up over the head and down the other side. Figure 13 shows the shims in position.

Now roll a strip of linoleum into a cylinder and tie it together. The cylinder should be just large enough to clear the shims, top and sides. Then stand the figure on a board and place the cylinder over it.

It is important to remember to seal the bottom of the linoleum cylinder to the board with plasticine or other clay. Otherwise, the plaster will run out underneath the linoleum.

Mix some plaster and fill the cylinder. Let it dry out for at least a day.

Remove the linoleum and with a hammer and thin chisel (an old wood chisel is ideal) carefully pry open the plaster. Because of the shims, it will break neatly into two halves. Remove the plasticine figure.

You now have a mold for casting a figure. Let this mold dry out thoroughly.

Next get a piece of household soap and a knife and half fill a cup with soap shavings. Pour some hot water on the shavings to fill the cup, and stir until the soap is dissolved. Let this mixture cool down and then paint the whole of the inside of the mold with it, including the outside edges. Let it dry and then do it once again. Sizing the mold with soap in this way prevents the fresh plaster from sticking to it.

Now bind the two halves of the mold strongly together with rope or thick string. They must be really firmly joined or plaster may seep out between the joints.

When this is done, turn the mold upside down, mix some plaster, and fill the mold with it.

After pouring the plaster into the mold, knock the mold gently on the table to settle the plaster in any corners and to free air bubbles.

When the plaster is dry, undo the rope and carefully remove the mold.

With a more complicated figure, where the removal of the mold by this means would mean damaging the cast figure, another method must be used.

Proceed as before, but color the plaster that you pour into the mold. Let this plaster dry out well.

14. Method of casting plaster blocks for carving

The mold must then be chipped away with a chisel. As the colored plaster becomes exposed, you will know you should take extra care. This is called waste-mold casting, because the mold is used only once.

MAKING BLOCKS FOR CARVING
You can also make plaster blocks for carving.

15. *Finished plaster shield and clay tiles. The hexagonal tiles were imprinted with designs from paper drawings*

Make the mold for blocks from wood, linoleum, or thick cardboard. Plastic containers are also suitable. Cylinders of plaster can be cast in these and the plastic cut away afterward. Since plastic is rather slippery, be careful when cutting it.

Mix the plaster to a creamy thickness, pour it into the molds, and bang them on the worktable to settle the plaster. Let it dry out, remove the molds, and you have your blocks ready for carving.

An old penknife makes a useful carving tool. Linoleum-cutting tools are handy for gouging. Various grades of sandpaper glued to pieces of wooden dowel are good for smoothing the finished carving.

3. Papier-mâché Modeling

MATERIALS AND TOOLS

Papier-mâché modeling is probably the most inexpensive method of modeling, and surprisingly good results can be achieved with it.

Papier-mâché work can be of three kinds; it can be done by using layers of paper and paste, pulp, or a commercial preparation.

Almost any kind of paper is all right, and you can use it with wallpaper paste, flour paste, and hot carpenter's glue, depending on the type of work.

A few tools are necessary: a pair of scissors, a sharp knife, and a pair of pliers if you are using wire.

You will also need a grease such as Vaseline.

THE LAYER METHOD

Modeling over ready-made objects
Different kinds of paper can be used for different kinds

of work. For example, a small model is best made with tissue paper and a thin paste. For a very large model thick brown paper and hot glue may be best.

Let us begin with a small object, say, a bulb bowl.

Place the bowl upside down over a tin can or something similar to raise it off the worktable. Grease the outside of the bowl with Vaseline.

Cut a number of tissue-paper squares, roughly an inch and a half square, and put a layer of them over the Vaseline. Take care to overlap each square with the one following it, and use more Vaseline if necessary to make the tissue stick.

Mix some paste. Wallpaper paste is clean to use and keeps well. A teaspoonful to a cup and a half of water is about right.

Soak some newspaper in water, wring it out, and tear it into small squares. Paste a layer of these squares over the greased tissue paper.

Now paste a layer of tissue-paper squares over the newspaper squares. Keep on with this, alternating with newspaper and tissue paper, until you have put on four layers of each.

Let the pasted layers come over the rim of the bowl; they can be trimmed level when dry.

When the eight layers of paper and paste are completed, go over them with your fingers and paste, smoothing down any unevenness. To make the bowl stronger, simply add more layers of paper and paste.

Let the paste dry out. Trim the edges and then remove

the model from the bowl. The model will come away easily if the Vaseline layer has been put on properly. Should you tear the model on removing it, it can easily be mended with tissue paper and paste.

To make it a neat job, seal the cut edges of the model with tissue paper and paste; two thicknesses of tissue will be enough.

A design can then be drawn on the bowl and painted.

A model can also be made by using the inside of the bowl instead of the outside. The method is the same except that the bowl can now stand upright on the work-table.

16. Modeling over a jar with papier-mâché

A straw holder can be made over a jam jar. If you wish, it can be made entirely of tissue paper and paste. Grease the outside of the jar and put on a layer of tissue without paste (see Figure 16). Cover about three quarters of the height of the jar. It can be trimmed down later when you have taken the model off the jar.

Modeling over balloons

This is the most interesting way to model papier-mâché. You can work with tissue paper or newspaper or with both, alternating the layers. When using newspaper, first let it soak in water, then wring it out, so that it is damp when you use it. This helps the paste to pene-

17. Modeling over balloons

39

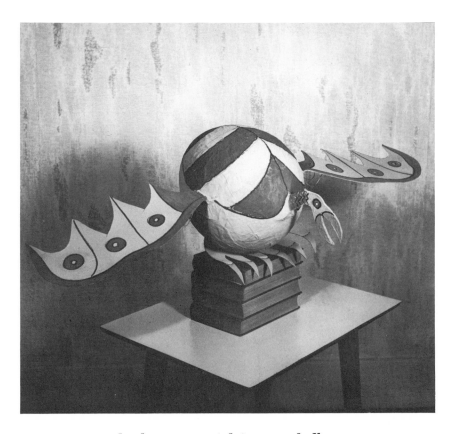

18. Imaginary bird: papier-mâché over a balloon

trate the paper more easily.

Depending on the size of the balloon you are using, cut or tear squares of paper of a convenient size for pasting, but do not make them too large.

Paste the squares right to the balloon. Overlap each square by the one following it, and make sure that the paste soaks into the paper.

Two colors of paper should be used to ensure an even coverage, or two different papers such as tissue and newspaper. It helps you to notice more readily any place that might have been missed. In the case of newsprint, use the pictures for one layer of squares and the print for the next layer.

Again, depending on the size of the balloon, the number of layers will vary, but from six to eight should be enough for most sizes.

19. Head mask: papier-mâché over a balloon

41

When you have completed all the layers and they are dry, the balloon can either be left to perish or it can be burst by pushing a pin into the model.

The model can now be used as a base. It can be made into a fish, a face, a mask, or an imaginary creature such as a large bird or an insect (see Figure 18).

For a mask that is to be worn choose a large balloon that will give a shape big enough to fit over the head of the person it is intended for. One end of the papier-mâché model has to be cut away. Tissue paper can serve as hair (see Figure 19).

Use card, wire, plastic foam, and other materials to make fins for fish, legs for animals, eyebrows and moustaches for faces, and so on. The papier-mâché will become hard enough to cut with a knife, so you can glue in cardboard fins, for example.

Joins can be sealed and hidden with a layer or two of tissue paper and paste.

It helps to give the finished model a coat of white paint. Then whatever you wish to paint on it can be drawn first in soft pencil or charcoal.

Modeling on wire mesh

Chicken wire or any other suitable wire mesh can be used to make large figures and decorations with layer papier-mâché.

Suppose, for example, you want to make a series of shields to hang on a wall. First make a pattern from card-

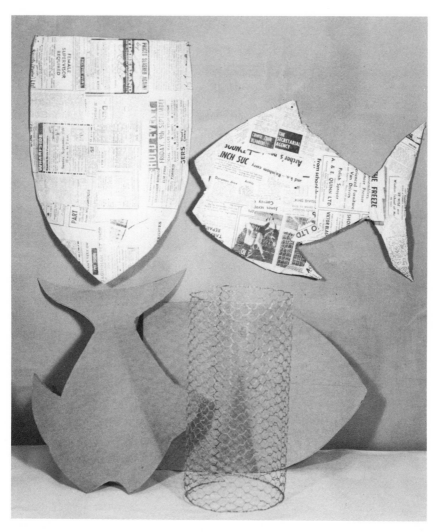

20. Modeling over wire mesh with patterns

board. Lay it over a piece of mesh and cut around the pattern with a wire cutter.

The mesh is then covered with layers of damp newspaper and paste until the required thickness is obtained. Edges should be carefully and evenly made by folding the paper over onto the back of the mesh.

21. Finished papier-mâché shield

44

When the papier-mâché is dry, it can be trimmed and any bad edges made good with more paper and paste.

You will find that you can bend the finished model into a shieldlike curve.

Give the surface of the shield a coat of white paint, and when it is dry, you can work out a design on it.

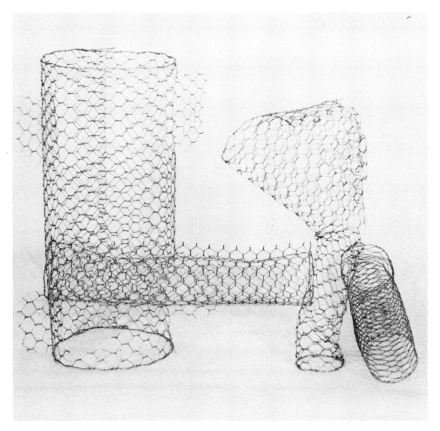

22. Preparing wire mesh for figure work

This type of papier-mâché work can be applied to many kinds of wall decoration, such as large flowers, fish, and masks.

You can even make life-size figures of people and

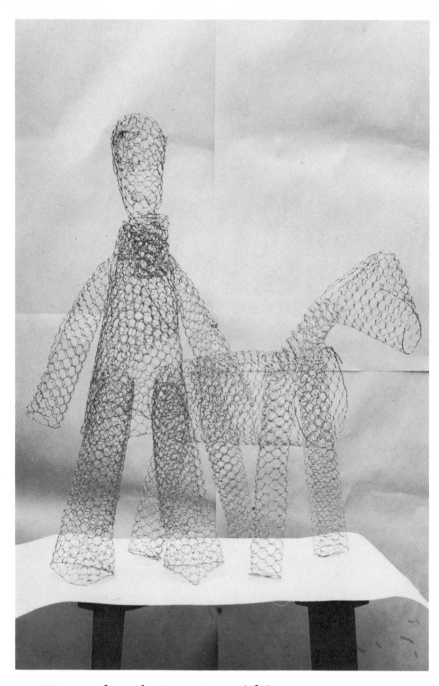

23. Wire mesh ready for papier-mâché

24. Covering wire mesh with layer papier-mâché

47

25. *Finished figures made from wire mesh and layer papier-mâché*

animals by using wire mesh and layers of paper and paste.

The mesh has to be cut first and bent to near the shape of the figure you want to make. In Figures 22 and 23 you will see how cylinders of wire mesh have been cut and slightly shaped into figures. Padding of paper can be used to fill in gaps and then covered with paste and paper (see Figure 24).

Puppet heads and dolls

With plasticine you can make models for puppet heads, to be covered with paper and paste. These will make excellent light glove puppets.

A piece of plasticine about twice the size of your fist gives you a good-size head. If the plasticine is hard, drop it into some warm water for a while to soften it. Dry it when you take it out of the water.

You can make a small modeling stand from a piece of broomstick about six inches long, nailed or screwed to a wooden base. Otherwise, the neck of a suitable bottle will do.

Break off part of the plasticine for use afterward as features, and roll the rest into a ball. Place the ball on top of the modeling stand and press it down to fashion a head and a neck. Make the neck as wide as your first two fingers. When the puppet is finished, these two fingers will go inside the neck.

With the plasticine you put aside, make the features on the face—that is, the eyes, nose, ears, lips, chin, and

26. Puppet head, bowl, and doll: layer papier-mâché

cheeks. Weld the plasticine together with fingers and thumbs. Do not make the features too thin or they will break off when you put on the papier-mâché.

When the head is ready, grease it with Vaseline and cover it with squares of tissue paper. Paste another six to eight layers of damp newspaper and tissue paper over this. Take care to press in the layers to the shape of the features and the head.

When the papier-mâché is dry, cut it in half to remove it. Put the point of the knife in the top of the head and cut down through the ear on one side. Then cut through the other side. Remember to trim around the bottom of the neck before doing this.

Lift off the two halves. Remove any Vaseline tissue

from the inside and rejoin the halves by putting some liquid glue along the edges of the cuts and pressing the halves together until the glue is dry. Then seal the join with two more layers of tissue paper and paste.

When this is dry the head is ready for painting.

Dolls can also be made in this way. Make a figure from plasticine over an armature, grease it, and continue as above. To remove the papier-mâché doll from the plasticine, cut around the sides and wherever else is necessary to remove the doll without breaking part of it. For example, it may be necessary to make cuts on the inside of the arms and legs in order to remove them cleanly. Try to make the doll come apart in halves. Then rejoin the halves with glue and paper and paste as for the puppet head.

27. *Method of removing papier-mâché figures from mold*

The simple doll in Figure 28 is like the Japanese Daruma doll. These are still made in Japan, and are

28. Finished papier-mâché models

supposed to be good luck. Sometimes they are sold without eyes. The idea is to paint in one eye and then, if your luck turns out good, to paint in the other eye. A feature of these dolls is that when you push them over they stand up straight again.

It is quite easy to make one of them. First, model the shape in plasticine: a pearlike shape. Grease it, put on tissue-paper squares, and follow with about eight layers of tissue and paste.

When the model is dry, cut it in three. Cut off the base to a depth of about half an inch, and cut down each side, beginning at the top. The base is filled with plaster. Let the plaster dry, remove it from the base, and then glue it back into position. Rejoin the model with glue, and seal the joins with paper and paste. Brick-red is the color sometimes used for these dolls, with the face painted white.

THE PULP METHOD

Making pulp

There are several ways to make papier-mâché pulp, which is useful for certain kinds of models. The simplest way is to tear newspaper into very small pieces, the smaller the better, and let it soak in water for twenty-four hours. Drain off as much of the water as possible and add paste to the paper. Flour paste can be added directly without mixing it; wallpaper paste must be mixed beforehand.

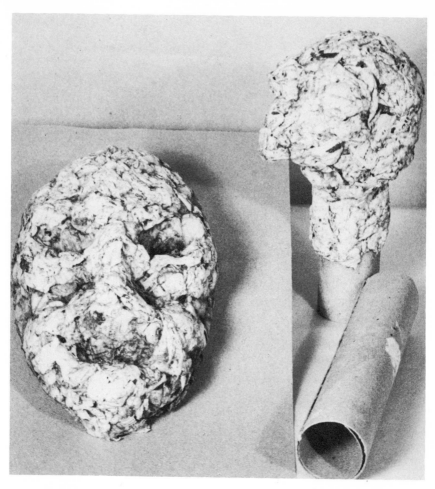

29. Mask form and puppet head from pulp papier-mâché

The paste and paper are then thoroughly mixed and left to stand for an hour or two.

Another method is to use crepe paper, flour, and salt. Cut the crepe paper into really small pieces and soak them in water for an hour or two. By the way, use white crepe paper to avoid staining your hands.

Strain off the water and add flour and salt to the soaked paper. The measurements are a cupful of flour and two tablespoons of salt to a piece of crepe paper about six feet long.

Knead this mixture to a doughlike substance and it is ready for modeling.

Papier-mâché pulp can be used for making forms for masks. The mask shape is made in pulp papier-mâché and allowed to dry. Then it is greased and gone over with layer papier-mâché. The mask can then be lifted off the form and another one made on the same form.

Puppet heads can be modeled with pulp. Make a cylinder out of cardboard or cut in half one of those rollers on which paper towels or aluminum foil are wound. Fashion the pulp over this cylinder (see Figure 29).

Relief maps showing hills, mountains, valleys, rivers, etc. can be made as a project for geography by first building up a base from cardboard and glue, and then going over it with pulp paper-mâché.

Any containers, such as buckets, should be cleaned immediately after the pulp has been made in them, since it is difficult to remove the paper and paste once it is dry.

4. Notes

A NOTE ON FIRING CLAY

As was said at the beginning of this book, the clay used for the modeling described in it is a clay that does not have to be fired. When a clay model is fired, it is put into an oven called a kiln and subjected to a great heat. After the model is removed from the kiln it is usually decorated with special paints and glazes, and then returned to the oven for a further heating to make the decoration permanent.

If you know someone with a kiln who will fire models for you, the clay to use is sculpture or ceramic clay for firing. This makes harder and therefore more durable models.

Before modeling, this clay has to be well kneaded and wedged. Wedging is the process of repeatedly cutting the clay in half and kneading it together again in order to get rid of air bubbles. Air bubbles in clay that is to be fired would cause the clay to crack under heat.

A TURNTABLE

When you have clay models to paint, a small turntable is most handy. Excellent turntables can be made from old phonographs, which can occasionally be picked up cheaply at junk stores.

Remove the turntable and its socket from the phonograph. Set the socket in a sturdy wooden base and make a plywood disc to cover the turntable. Models can be placed on this for painting and need not be disturbed while it is being done.

SOURCES OF MATERIAL

Clay.   Boneware Self-hardening Clay needs no firing. It is put out by Sculpture House, Inc., 38 East 30th Street, New York, New York, 10016. Other self-hardening clays can be bought in stores selling artists' materials. Also available in these stores is a clay that can be fired in a kitchen oven at 250° F. Stewart Clay Company, Inc., 133 Mulberry Street, New York, New York, 10013, manufactures such a clay under the brand name of Ceraclay. It comes in a dry or moist form.

Glue.   Elmer's Glue and Duco Cement are good, strong glues that can be used for many things in model making. Clay models that meet with an accident can be neatly restored with these glues.

Paint.   Della Robbia Liquid Glaze, which is put out by Sculpture House, is an excellent paint, but almost any can be used to decorate the models in this book.

Tempera powder paints mixed with starch are good. The starch gives the paint body and fixes it so it won't rub off. You can buy large plastic bottles of liquid starch in the supermarket.

Papier-mâché.   A commercial product that is shredded and ready to use with water is available from Sculpture House, Inc. or at artists' supply stores. One brand name is Fybra Mix, which is manufactured by Stewart.

Paste.   Wallpaper paste, which is easy to make and clean to use, can, of course, be bought at shops selling wallpaper.

Plaster.   White Casting Plaster is available at most large art-supply stores or can be ordered from Sculpture House, Inc. Plaster of Paris will do just as well, however. It is inexpensive and can be bought in a hardware store.

Plasticine.   Plasticine is a permanently plastic modeling clay that can be bought in one-pound blocks under various trade names at art stores or ordered from Sculpture House, Inc., where it is called Plasteline.

Wire.   Different gauges of galvanized wire can be bought at hardware stores. This is a pliable wire sold in handy rolls. It is useful for making armatures.

Wire mesh.   This is normally used for making chicken runs or to stop small dogs from getting through fences. The size of the mesh varies. Half-inch mesh was used for the models in this book. It can be bought at hardware stores, as can screen wire.

Books for Further Reading

Books for Further Reading

Anderson, Mildred. *Papier-Mâché and How to Use It.* Sterling Publishing Company, 1964.

Duncan, Julia H. and D'Amico, Victor. *How to Make Pottery and Ceramic Sculpture.* Museum of Modern Art, New York, 1947. Distributed by Simon & Schuster.

Haggar, Reginald G. *Pottery Through the Ages.* Roy Publishers, 1959.

Paine, Roberta M. *Looking at Sculpture.* Lothrop, Lee & Shepard, 1968.

Zarchy, Harry. *Ceramics.* Alfred A. Knopf, 1954.

Index

Index

INDEX

Animals
   clay, 13, 14, 15
   papier-mâché, 45, 48*, 49
   plaster, 29*
Armature, 10, 20, 21*, 27-28,
   28*, 29*, 51, 58
Ashtrays, clay, 13
Balloons, modeling over,
   39*, 39-42, 40*, 41*
Blocks, plaster, 33*, 34-35
Bowls, clay
   from a coil, 15, 15*
   from a cube, 13
   from a sphere, 13*
Bowls, papier-mâché, 37-38,
   50*
Casting, *see* Figure casting.

* *Indicates illustration*

Ceraclay, 57
Clay
   Boneware Self-hardening,
   9, 57
   sculpture and ceramic, 56
Coils, clay models from,
   14-15, 15*
Cones, clay models from, 14
Cubes, clay models from,
   11-13
Della Robbia Liquid Glaze,
   57
Designs
   on clay, 11, 12, 14, 17,
   18, 34*
   on papier-mâché, 45
   on plaster, 23, 25, 28
Dolls
   clay, 14

62